WHIRL IS KING

Louisiana State University Press
Baton Rouge

WHIRL
IS KING

POEMS FROM A LIFE LIST

Brendan Galvin

NATIONAL
ENDOWMENT
FOR THE ARTS

*This publication is supported in part by an award
from the National Endowment for the Arts.*

PUBLISHED BY LOUISIANA STATE UNIVERSITY PRESS
Copyright © 2008 by Brendan Galvin
All rights reserved
Manufactured in the United States of America

Designer: Michelle A. Neustrom
Typefaces: ITC Century, Impressum

LIBRARY OF CONGRESS CATALOGING-IN-PUBLICATION DATA

Galvin, Brendan.
  Whirl is king : poems from a life list / Brendan Galvin.
    p. cm.
  ISBN 978-0-8071-3349-1 (cloth : alk. paper) — ISBN 978-0-8071-3350-7 (pbk. : alk. paper)
  I. Title.
  PS3557.A44W47 2008
  811'.54—dc22

                                                              2007046067

Some of the poems in this collection originally appeared in *Habitat: New and Selected Poems,
1965–2005* (Baton Rouge: Louisiana State University Press, 2005); *Place Keepers* (Baton Rouge:
Louisiana State University Press, 2003); *The Strength of a Named Thing* (Baton Rouge: Louisiana
State University Press, 1999); *Sky and Island Light* (Baton Rouge: Louisiana State University Press,
1996); *Great Blue: New and Selected Poems* (Urbana: University of Illinois Press, 1990); *Wampanoag
Traveler* (Baton Rouge: Louisiana State University Press, 1989); *Winter Oysters* (Athens: University
of Georgia Press, 1983); *Atlantic Flyway* (Athens: University of Georgia Press, 1980); and *The
Minutes No One Owns* (Pittsburgh: University of Pittsburgh Press, 1977).

    And in these magazines: *Alaska Quarterly Review, Amicus Journal, Atlantic Monthly,
Chronicles, Crab Orchard Review, Crazyhorse, Flyway, Georgia Review, Idaho Review, Kenyon
Review, Laurel Review, Missouri Review, The New Criterion, New England Review, New Yorker,
Northeast Magazine, Poetry, Quarterly West, Sewanee Review, Shenandoah, Southern Review,
Tar River Poetry,* and *Three Rivers Poetry Journal.*

The paper in this book meets the guidelines for permanence and durability of the Committee on
Production Guidelines for Book Longevity of the Council on Library Resources. ∞

For Maddie, while she can still fly

During southerly migrations, up to 12 million birds leave Cape Cod per night.
—*Scientific American*

....

In a world older and more complete than ours they move finished and complete, gifted with extensions of the senses we have lost or never attained, living by voices we shall never hear. They are not brethren, they are not underlings; they are other nations, caught with ourselves in the net of life and time, fellow prisoners of the splendor and travail of the earth.
—HENRY BESTON, *The Outermost House*

....

If a blackpoll warbler were burning gasoline instead of body fat, it could boast of getting 720,000 miles to the gallon.
—*Scientific American*

....

Whirl is king.
—ARISTOPHANES, *The Clouds*

Contents

WHIRL IS KING

SKYLIGHTS

Every October, after a day when something
exotic has landed at the feeder
and waits gasping there as on a prow
far out at sea, a myrtle or Canada warbler
just too wing-beaten to go on,
I wake late to a good dinner
building its cloud above my heart,
and look up where stars in the skylight
on that night alone have a connect-the-dots logic,
a plan I might follow that's pressing
like a template in my head. Then I envision
the great streaming freeways of the birds,
those swerves and swoopings in every
color of feather, three miles up, blurred
Crayola streaks a hemisphere long, and
Surinam, French Guiana, Venezuela
loom in a summer down there
like the eminence of a new green heart.
I play around with gravity and magnetic
lines of force trined with the pull of the moon,
but panic hearing the surf of a different
coast in each ear, and drop to name
real hills instead: Tom's and Cathedral
enfolding an arm of river between
bay and ocean; Round and Corn, between
the freshwater lens my pump taps into
and those stars. Husband, father to sleepers,
doorman to dogs, I can't convert pasta
to vector energy anyway. I might say
something I ate causes this,
and tip an invisible nightcap
to the birds, who know where they're going
and how to get there.

GREAT BLUE

Often,
around certain backwaters
like the ponds behind the oyster shacks,
I hope for a heron,

and sometimes I'm granted
that wood-silver,
crooked-stick, channel-marker effect
of the loosened neck,

and that silence, humped like
an overburden of experience,
the weight it hauls in flight
from river to pond above a highway

when I look up at the mere
abstract silhouette *bird* but am taken
by the dragged beat of wings

translucent at their tips,
and the cocked spurs trawled behind,
and have to swerve to hold the lane.

But I never expected it this morning,
Mother, on the wall of this room
you share with strangers:

the Egyptian sign for the generation
of life, its wisp of feather
hairlike off the nape, among the old
in their own humped solitudes.

Reason, that chain-store item,
can deny this forever, but that bird
shadows us, at key moments is there,

its gumped-up look guarding justice,
longevity, the journey
of the good and diligent soul.

A FEW LOCAL NAMES OF THE
DOUBLE-CRESTED CORMORANT

This is the fishbird that flew here
directly out of its fossil imprint, unchanged
for sixty million years, hell's turkey
from its punk hairdo to its black rubber
scuba-flipper feet, hanging its wingspread
to dry on rocks and creek banks, crosstrees
of masts, the insignia of a country that has
no plans for peace and no word for civility,
nesting in branches of matted seaweed
this guano goose fixes in a mixture
of its own trashfish paste and pellets,
until the tree surrenders of chagrin
and collapses to poison its pond. It is all
overstatement, stink duck and goo loon,
and can make a buffet of a catfish farmer's
ponds, then slime every deck in the harbor
with the by-product overnight, collateral
damage, its green mineral eyechip
and yellow gawp testimony that it knows
it has thrived beyond dinosaurs
and will slip past even the cockroaches
on its own slicks, this gluebird,
stool pigeon, shag rat.

A MILE DOWN THE ROAD FROM HOME

I've caught myself
whistling a bumpy version
of "Take the A Train," and only
because this catbird
in a beachplum thicket has
taken me up on it
or close enough, the bird
keeping a breath or two behind
as if trying to hear where
I'm taking him, then diving
back into his own songline,
improvising along his strung-out
warbles and gutturals, and now
a few kingfisher rattles
and perhaps a black-billed cuckoo
or something else he's brought
up the hemisphere for this
season of courtship, cackles
and chucks, even a treefrog's piping.
I can feel Darwin frowning over me
like a thunderhead. A little
shaky about messing around
in natural selection, I look
both ways, taking care the bird
and I are alone before I donate
a ragged thread from *Peter Grimes*
to this slate-colored, black-capped
male who has only
a rufous undertail for flash.

WALTER ANDERSON SLEEPING ON THE LEVEE

In New Orleans to research Hurricane Betsy,
the one he'd ridden out tied to a tree trunk
on Horn Island, he rolled up for the night
on the levee by Audubon Park, letting
the Mississippi talk him to sleep.
Surrounded again, as on the island,
toward morning he felt the serious eyes,
and waited on the moment they'd show themselves.
He saw for the one and only time
the carcasson, then the smaragdine
and gallowglass, but were these the names
of birds, or the names of birds
he wished there were? If a bird is a hole
in heaven through which a man may pass,
then what in the hell were all these anxious
steppers? No pouldeau or pelican, nothing
he'd ever sketched or done in watercolors,
no redwing or boat-tailed grackle
that waited for raisins and cold rice
he'd fling them from last night's supper.
The hurricane, he figured, had lifted
these strangers out of the park's aviary.
Could they sense that he'd talked with
the morning star, or escaped from hospitals
because authority amused him? He was
necessary again: on the levee these birds
would starve or be brought down by
an air rifle or household beast. Casting
breadcrumbs over his shoulder, he led them
back into the park, wrestling their names
from himself, pied piper of the stonechuck
and pripet, the fireneck, peabill,
mer-hen, the garget, the stant.

YOUNG OWLS

Now crows mill blackly above them,
yawking as though
something is stuck in their craws,
and a panic of baby white
floats off the nest as if
struck in midflight.

But they are there,
trying deficient wings
and feet like goalies' mitts
at the nest's brink,
trying a gargle of little bones
and a stare like corpse candles,
their black pupils fixed in yellow.

They sit it out,
or lean into the future,
waiting for their buff feathers
to straggle downhill through scrub
till they are dressed like bark.

Visitations of neither
luck nor wisdom, they mean
no frogs in the garden this year,
no hunting the slope under the nest
for lady slippers
languorous with spring.

Dropping to berry tangles
on feet that later, quicker,
will snatch June bugs from the air
and flip them like popcorn
to their beaks,
they waddle toward dusk

and clutches of young terns
in the hollows on Egg Island,

fuzzy about how shadows
drop out of the sun,
how nothing in this world
gets out of its life alive.

ONE FOR THE LIFE LIST

Not a yellowthroat,
not a yellow warbler, but a
yellow-throated warbler—
it has happened again: the sky
moving out of the west
and before the clouds
migrants come scudding,
so many so fast that the pines
are mobile with blue backs
and bay breasts switching places,
undertail coverts flicking
yellow, white, twitching among
branches, impossible to locate
fast enough, but as though
at the end of summer
an East European primitivist
had painted a Christmas tree
whimsical with birds.
A yellow-throated warbler, one
for the life list, though
I promised myself again
I'd swear off this year.
Instead I've come back
for just one more, a failed
teetotaler of birds,
and better this stupefaction at
a lemon-bibbed ounce of
feathers than the shoddy
illusion of the aloneness
of things, wherein the sky
pours down oceanic emptiness
and the life of a grove migrates
across the road to the gas pumps:
even the common foreground
chickadee and background crow
give dimension to our days,

and not to salute such
charity of song
though it be plain as
thumbsqueaks on clear windowpanes,
not to say their names,
and the shadow of death passes
across our tongues.

INTERVENTIONS

Smoking an Upmann Lonsdale
from Havana, drinking a pint
of Guinness, I sat in the November sun
watching a late dragonfly, golden
in her chapel-window wings.

It seemed necessary to declare
the half-life of happiness until
that bug ended it in my glass
and I remembered the little hawk,

outside on its back, blue-gray,
its head rocking gently, talons
straight out in shock-splay, a calm
on its face no subtle hook could change,
and the window still there.

I'd seen it around, a merlin
by its tail stripes, conducting some
terrible interventions: once,
when I knelt on the path to cup
a grounded warbler I thought
had stunned itself against glass,

something proprietary came
almost to hand in a slate-colored
U-turn and beat it for the woods;
and once, out of the pines with a twist
it picked a sparrow off a bush and back

into the pines so quick it left a contrail
a few seconds on the air. Its feet
in a death-clutch now, I saw
the fish-eyed glaze, the head-on
flight shape dusting a window.

CHICKADEE

The crow is only an anvil,
and the goldfinches' song
can be duplicated by rubbing
the right sticks together.
Next to yours
the blue feet of titmice
are merely a fad.

There are jays with voices
full of elbows
in my world, too,
dragoons on leave,
who appear to have molted
all the way to their head points.

But you, minimal wingbeat,
you're there, not there:
the economy of your arrival
puts a whole squad
of evening grosbeaks to shame.

I believe that other puritan
was looking at you when
he first thought, "Beware of
enterprises that require
new clothes."

I've believed in your way
since that evening
the owl sat
waiting for light to drain
into dusk, and you
flew straight in

and, seeing him there,
at the last instant
dipped up just enough,
and taught me
the duende of chickadees.

PELICAN

That look of a singular relic
blown out of the annals
of evolution, such mock-seriousness
turned loose on this world
they might have dubbed me
"Pelican" as early as high school,

not merely for my addiction
to wharves and my vertigo
out of sight of tidal habitats,
but for broad-flippered feet
that still make me
hard to follow on dance floors,

and for the way, late at night,
trying to make it home
in my black Filene's Basement
clerical trenchcoat (but lined in
cardinal red!), I'd flap
a few strokes, then sail and
flap a few more, the whole getup
assembled to suggest
a saving naïveté.

Then there's my approach to
necessity, not the direct sharp
plunge of a gannet, all torque
to an economical vanish, but
the splash of some bulk
a deckhand rolls over the side
as soon as land
has cleared the horizon.

If they stuck around
after that splatter, they'd have
seen it was all in knowing

the exact angle for entry,
sheer technique so I come up
sitting every time, making
those swallowing movements
that ensure I will never
go hungry, operating on
too many levels at once,
the usual crowd of laughing gulls
hanging around for crumbs.

THE MOCKINGBIRD

Far into moonlight he tries
to recall his own song,
but a whippoorwill
floats out three notes
wobbly and clear as bubbles,
so he corrects them for her,
melding them with a child's
creaky swing, but erases
that line, and takes a new tack
from a siren on Route 17,
then drops to a cowbird
like water poured into water.

This business of getting
the world right
isn't for dilettantes; when
the voices fill you,
you must say nothing wrong,
but follow them back
through the day, going phrase
by phrase over hills,

pausing here and there on a pole
to help goldfinches chip
the sun to a perfect wheel,
dropping by underleaf stones
to improve on mandalas
a cricket's printing in air,
and waiting at cedar posts
to teach killdeer
to pronounce their own names better.

You must bring it all back
alive as the repertoire
of your inner ear,
past fences and over stones,

through one face of leaves
and another
to someone awake on the outskirts,
this woman propped on a pillow,
beginning to see, among fifes,
in her darkened room,
a band dressed like Blue Caballeros.

You must help her imagine
sun living on brass horns,
and an easy, foot-saving march
as the ensemble passes,
air in its wake
banged to a bass difference.

GLASS

What the warbler must have seen
was the world swung round;
without turning back
she was flying into
a distance already passed through:

another side of the woodpile
she had just cleared in a single pitch,
and beyond, through the middle ground
of pines, the background glitter
of running sea she had skipped above
like a flat stone thrown so well
it touches down on water
all the way to the other shore.

Swung round,
only slightly blurred.
Trees twinning,
far water grained,
air of a density . . .

then that split-second insight

into splashes of newspaper
and clothing,
filtered through
final dusts of light.

As perhaps,
in our last seconds,
we are swung round
to live ourselves back through
each particular,
to fall faster and faster
out of loves, out of
changes of clothes,

whole snows lifting skyward
becoming autumn leaves lifting
back into green trees,
the dead stepping out of
crumbling loam,

at the last, seed and egg
unraveling, falling away.

And all
in the time
it takes a flat stone to skip over water
and be let in.

WHITE-THROAT

Maybe the conflagration is touched off each year
when the first matchhead of a crocus flares,
which no one ever sees, but here in the planter
on the railing is a white-throated sparrow,

looking ragged as something a chef
just threw in a rage at an exhaust fan,
a peabody bird bathing in icemelt,
sending its golden droplets up as though
seeding the sunlight, not a crocus yet in sight.

So this is the source of those controlled
burns of forsythia by our houses
two weeks in April, lanterns in the drawn-out
noirs of fog, lights private as ships at sea, whereby
the mailman navigates from house to house.

A long time before we'll hear
Old Sam Peabody, Peabody, Peabody,
but immersed in total pleasure for at least
five minutes now, splashing itself, feet sunk
in the planter's mud, this bird knows the water

will freeze again, and maybe that everything
coming after—even lilacs, and shadbush ghosting
among unlit trees—depends on these yellows
it's flipping into being with its wings.

For bracts and mayapples, for a goldfinch
knocking at a window's conundrum,
this white-throat's whipping up the sunlit modulations,
sulfur, citrines, gilt, canary, amber,

for pollen, and month to month across monotonous greens,
for the wings of fritillaries thinner than onionskin,
until seaside goldenrod gathers and concentrates
saffron, packing it in for cold storage.

BELOW THE HILL OF THE THREE CHURCHES

The little oyster dragger swings out
on its hawser as far right
as the first flat run of tide in the channel
allows. It panics a frieze of willets into
running left away from its hull, or else
the hull is still and the shifting birds
suggest motion to it, as a ship departing
will seem to set the pier underway; but now
the dragger's tending left where a
smoke-light skein of least sandpipers
just landed, a shoal creeping forward as
the willets step right, stiff-legged,
mimicking that bridge crossing mud on stilts
far down where a gull begins to slide
on a crawl of heat among exposed hummocks.
Taken with its own effortless riding, it
spins this way on the silt-lift, now that.
Come quick out the door of the Feed and
Grain and ground me with a sack of
sunflower seeds: under three spires
I'd believed rigid until now,
everything's deviating from the mean.

A RING OF QUAIL BONES

I found them just off the fireroad
by the marsh, around a low
bush of wind-stripped sweet gale,
breastbones like plowshares,
skulls papery, still unscuffled where
they'd crouched in their circle,
heads outward, still facing
whatever night brings, ready
to explode up the air
that found them out and feathered them
a flake at a time and left them under
rain and crust. This morning,
my gaze drawn upward by a muffled
thump at the skylight, three
drank on yellow feet
from a gathered night rain,
their bellies patterned with arrowheads,
another little drama of the fall;
and certain gifts from childhood
occurred, models of perfection I had
no fingers fine enough to assemble.

THE GRACKLES

From a dream of armor collapsing,
the clatter of helmets and greaves,
gauntlets crashing on stone,

I woke knowing they were back,
their cries gleaned from homestead gates
the wind on the northern rim
of America toys with.

If it were only one or a few
such as all summer scuffled
in the huckleberry,

their failed storekeeper's eyes—
worry trapped in a bile-yellow
ring of anger—taking the inventory
of underleaf lives,

but this morning so many moved so fast
from pokeweed to cutworm to acorns
they eluded count, outriders
flaked off a southgoing cloud,

their feathers amalgamating steel-blue
and bronze, as though every bird
had been dipped in a lubricant
intended to soothe its cries into song.

All day they split
the gross contents of pods, twangling
like so many cash drawers springing open,

hoarding all they could carry
for their long haul toward the evening's
vast collision, where they would provide
the final clatter of chrome.

FOR THE RAVEN'S RETURN

I keep checking out the North Pamet crows
for the Great Corvid who may slip into town
and wear that whole flock for his cloak.
I'll know him by his diamond-shaped tail
and the way he flies upside down, aerialist
above winter, the envy of grounded herons
puffed up against that gulag weather.

Raffish and disreputable, those old mariners
who lurch on the slippery cobbles in my sleep
understand and speak all sixty-four
variations of the quork to companion
ravens riding their shoulders.
That's how they keep those eyebright
hunters sitting there, ruffed out in blue-green
and warbling to themselves for an hour at a time
like introspective drunks.

Korax the Croaker should be welcomed this way,
those sailors tell me:
                              Out of everything
eastbound from Long Gone, bears on the beltway,
that moose on the library lawn, cougars, coyotes,
fishers, it's you we need most, whom no supervisor asks,
Why did you do it this way and not that way? Why were you
there yesterday when you should have been here?

From gilded perches in the capitols, our representatives
sing the lobbyists' tunes. Bring your reclusive talents
and replenish us with all you have learned in exile, Croaker,
for the steeple-crowned hats that ratified
your Old World repute and drove you out of here
have gone west themselves, and the roadkills
multiply, tributes and honoraria for you:
full moon raccoons, skunk courtships thwarted by
our interstates in the first week of February.

Make of these trees taking our cornfields back
your great hall again. Dumpsters multiply
for you across the land; inside the hollow steeples
of churches, the cell phone towers grow taller,
reaching for that year when no one will stand
in silence alone without punching the numbers in,
when no one will hanker to crack their wings
and fly around cronking.

A FOOTNOTE TO POWER

On a day so still you might think
that saying *wind* out loud
could start a crack the equinox
would ooze golden from,
I found a bolt on Corn Hill Road,

and weighed it in my hand,
feeling its otherworldly cold,
as though it had dropped
from the undercarriage of a cloud,

and listened to the nuthatch
telegraph in bushes whose maroon haze
signified their readiness
to begin again, a few natural egg cups
woven in them here and there,
abandoned but waiting.

Thick as my thumb and longer
than any teacup-sized warbler's nest
is deep, that heavy-duty piece
had an octagonal head on it

larger than any resting place
a hummingbird might bind
to the merest knuckle
of an apple tree, a steel bolt shaken
to unthreading, and fallen.

LETTER ACCOMPANYING THE SPECIMEN OF AN AMAZING BIRD, 1763

If shipboard rats
haven't worried this little beauty
out of condition entirely,
and it has escaped those meddlesome
sorts of sailors who jimmy shipments
with a nose for liquors preserving
specimens, you will see here
a thing which in your old world
has no counterpart. These sleep
all winter, though none among
the Wampanoags can tell me where.
In summer, when I myself so love
to nap in the influence of flowers,
I have been roused by a sudden
buzzy agitation in the bell of
a trumpetvine. At first nothing
is there, then one of these
flower birds, or bird flowers—
they are so ornamented—will fly
backwards out, as quick in
reverse motion as forward,
for they go up, down, sideways
and continuous, and can stand
upon air with only a minor arousal
of it, then brief and direct as
a shooting star proceed to
a grass-pink or trillium to siphon
fragrance through their tubular beaks,
thence perhaps to the lips
of the red turtlehead blossom.
I conclude that they live solely
upon these aromas, favoring
oranges and reds because their vapors
produce the most energy. You will
not be surprised to discover that

I have tried this airy diet myself,
and for days have gone about
without other sustenance, intruding
my nose in blooms, sniffing essences,
careful not to seal the exit of a bee
or whatever else, until my rebellious
appetite drove me to clean out
the cupboard. But would I could drive
the bung home on those fellows
in your country who pronounce upon
our stingy air and unfruitful weathers—
for here's a bird that thrives
upon them! Their own sky is but
a ceiling ringed with painted nymphs,
and could I drop one of those
shrimplings overboard, just as
a great ray is passing, its breadth
that of two gentlemen's cloaks,
it wouldn't fail to elevate
the hairs along his wretched neck.
Or if I could discover the means
of sending across to you a living moose,
its rack like a tree and so plattered
a banquet could be set upon it.
A herd of your deer could cavort
beneath its legs, and posed before it
you would make no more effect than
milady's lapdog. It is true we have
no ruins, no cathedrals, but therefore
no weight of history to wrestle
as a farmer his pasture stones,
only mountains that heave like ocean,
as fit as Sinai for receipt of
prophecy, sublime for the unfolding
of immortality, and waters upon
the landscape equal to a clear eye

in an honest face, and trees which,
were they men, would be grand
originals, models for busts
and frescoes worthy of log houses.
The specious politeness of your
enervated world we are without,
and its disguises. Would we cringe
like toads, our backs mimicking
leaves spotted with decay, not to
offend or disturb? Who meets
an American meets him square-toed,
square-faced in open air, nose out,
the prow of his countenance
broached to whatever weather.
But I am straying from my path again.
The scarlet wimple on the throat
of this bird seems black
in weak light. Other times it passes
through changes that emulate
the tinctures of those flowers it
loves best. I have watched
a female collecting milkweed silk
and down of ferns, saddling them
to an underleaf branch with stolen
spider web and the strings of
caterpillars, then implanting
this device with tree moss.
Hence the nest which I enclose,
its cup formed when the industrious
bird works her body down, fitting it
to the central mass, forming the cup
preparatory for these two eggs
or twin white beans, which are merely
seeds, perhaps more secret in
their processes, but led by the same
warmth and moisture to similar

increase of life. Mantises,
dragonflies, frogs, even
the gummy spider web are this humbird's
nemeses, though one of these
flying fractions will drive after
a crow with the persistence of
a winged auger. An early frost, too,
will stun them from the air
before they can make for winter sleep,
whereby I go about among the trees
collecting them like fruit.

CORNCRAKE

To take the rust off the needle
in its haystack, try this:
Isle of Lewis, Outer Hebrides,
a grown-over field on its north tip,
and a corncrake sounding somewhere in
knee-high grass like your thumb
run down the tines of a comb.
Elusive field-soul, quail-size
and feathered like the field, heard
less and less since tractors began
against the eggs' stillness.
Wade in and risk being taken for
a retired farmer, his plowhorse
sold, walking a straight furrow
as if hitched in the traces of dementia,
left to right and reversing all the way
into the depth of field, while this
voice thrower's there, now over
there, until the cliffs begin
and a few feet away kittiwakes turn
above ocean boiling on stone.
And the corncrake? Silent. Or gone,
though you've still never seen it fly.
The one right word in the whole
thesaurus of field may have crouched
between your feet as you passed
troubling the grass over it.

WRENS ON SHETLAND

Whatever sings bigger
than it is, when it isn't
merely talk, is worth
an afternoon, so I stood

among them while they built
in the stone walls, made
safe houses of moss
and pickup sticks, tucked
nest after nest mouselike

in a wrecked hull,
in knotholes, between a corn
oven's stones, pausing
only to twirl a loop of song,

working to exhaust whatever
in them trembles relentlessly
from beak's curvature to
tail overcocking.

They reproved me for standing
still by ignoring me,
as I ignored the flashier
bonxies, gannets, puffins
on the Noup, the rafts
of razorbills loafing offshore.

Then I saw they were saving
all they could of what
wind tears off things
it bends forever eastward

on those islands named like
wind-rush—Noss, Bressay,
Out Skerries—packing stray
sheepstuff and bog cotton
in, treading, working things

smooth as once they did
in the skull of Erland
Blacktooth, that blond
spreader of havoc.

AN INTERMISSION

After the last snows and the first
April chive-bursts, two came in
off the flyway, not flying
but coasting, humped to catch the air,
their wings on the long glide
without a single beat. White as if
a breeze were buffing fresh snowbanks,
their wing-sound was like wind
over snow—two tundra swans
by their black bills, not the decorative
imports children toss old bread at
on public water, but long as a man
and spanned wide as an eagle. Could
some epic I read forty years ago
have drawn them out of my mind
into the air? *Cygnus columbianus*,
named for the river Lewis and Clark
found them on, they had come
all the way from Currituck Sound
or the Chesapeake, aimed for
the high Arctic nesting grounds. Like gods
out of their element, they floated past me
above the pond and on down
the riverine marshes, pagan, twinned,
impersonal in their cold sublimity,
blind to my witness, their necks
outsnaking, intent on a brief rest
somewhere on our little river.

THE SOUTH UIST BUS

Outer Hebrides

He's a wee handy man, climbing
onto the bumper to whack the battery
into compliance with a stilson.
Now the little green bus turns over and begins
to lurch forward, and he settles it
into fifteen miles an hour. "A quarter
of a million on her," he says,
"and good for another." It's him and me,
and I'm here for the *machair*,
twenty miles of buttercups, orchids, vetch
and bird's-foot trefoil exuding a yellow haze
that floats just above the ground
the whole western length of the island,
the Atlantic beyond through lapses of dune.
Greenshank country, with snipe signing
the air in random whistling zigzags,
lapwings, redshanks, oystercatchers,
and the ruins of a second-century
wheelhouse at Kilphedar. He's here
because somebody in Ulster an eon ago
got tired of dodging Niall of the Nine Hostages
or his like, and rowed over one night
to discover fishing and farming
were more congenial to a long life.
One eye's on the road, one's studying
my rucksack and seventeen-pocket parka,
and he's no doubt wondering why anyone
would go into the *machair* except
to pasture cows. "Have a care if you get
up-island," he says. "The army may be
banging about on their missile range
today. Ach, I've sailed merchant marine
around the world, and they hate
the English everywhere." He'll stop
for anyone who can raise a hand,

at Howmore, by the corner of the road
to Ormaclete, near a house
glued all over with starbursts
of purple mussels and scallop shells,
"I'll be along" his only schedule.
They're old women mostly, heading off
for lochside houses, and one ancient couple,
joined by the handles of a plastic grocery bag,
all of them speaking "the Garlic,"
weather talk I'm guessing. "A hen harrier!"
I must have just shouted it, because I'm
the one pointing. And I'm the foolish one
when he wrestles the steering wheel
and pulls the bus over so I can take in
the silver male hawk circling the bog
and they can take me in, all of them smiling,
pleased I've come all the way from America
to admire their island, or else this
is how they handle the mad. The bird
sails off east toward the mountains.
"Thank you," I say to no one
and everyone, and back on the road
they're smiling and nodding at me,
speaking that poetry of conspirators,
and our driver says, "One of us
wants to know where a man
might buy a pair of boots like those."

NOSS

Shetland Islands

In yellow solipsist faces
the gannets stand around
on their slabs like Hyde Park cranks
orating to themselves in every
direction. Guillemots
shuffle for position, their formal
stag lines ledged on the cliff walls—
too much life and nothing that wants
you here on this island where humans
have thrived even less than trees.
At the point called Mansie's Berg
someone lived once, and Norsemen
named this bay Rumble Wick.
Walls the Shetland wrens flit
in and out of, feeding their young,
were laid a stone at a time
across this woolpatch texture of
peat, rock, sheep scat, wind,
and ocean sun—moorlands where
the new lambs bleat under cover
of eroded gullies, where fulmars
nesting on the edge
work their bull necks for offensive
oils when you come too near.
Solstice, and druids on Income
Support convene at Stonehenge,
mobilizing the police, but here
there are no fire-eaters
or jugglers, only kittiwakes
cruising your steps, then great
skuas coming in low enough
to rap your skull
with a fisted claw. Even the mild
wheatears seem outraged
at your stumbling on this mad

bird-birthing place of
the universe. It is all cackling,
whines, mewlings against
your presence, until one of
the meanings of islands
where the final hangers-on
petitioned for removal dawns on you,
and now you have a little litany
which goes, Noss, Taransay, Scarp,
Mousa, St. Kilda, to support you
toward some measure of humility.

LITTLE KING

I was up at the eaves on my ladder,
slipping cedar shingles under the trim
and trueing them to the chalkline,
three blows to each nail as you swept
around the apple trees and striped maple
in your golden crown, the only royalty
I'll allow here. As though to assure me
there's no hurry, you came out of leaden air
to glean the branches while I
collapsed deck chairs and fitted them
like a line of Rockettes into the shed. Advent:
things are drawing closer out of the leaves'
dissolution, rooftops, whole houses
reappearing across the marsh
whose grasses mimic the color spectrum
of wines. Last night a blond
fieldmouse fed at the suet when
I let the dog out, and today it's you,
my guest in this season of small things.
If I were a golden-crowned kinglet
I wouldn't have to search under pole beans
that resemble burnt wiring now,
hunting the winter squashes hiding there
as though they had a sense of humor,
piling the wheelbarrow full so I think
of cobblestones my grandfathers
moved in the same way. After the first
snow there's a second snow, so I hope
you'll take the rubythroat south
with you. It keeps returning to air
its sugar feeder hung in, and should have
crossed weeks ago to Yucatan.

UNDERSTORIES

Now from this island of deadfall
at the road's bend, the sudden
conflagration of an oriole's song.
What music in there among
the wind-broken and upstanding
pines and oaks, poplars
sprung through jagged breaks,
what nestings after the overtures
and proposals emanating from five kinds
of birdberry coverts, roses, catbrier
and fiddlehead tangles.

These thickets make a weir
for trapping wind-traveled seeds,
and on this May morning a shoal
off the flyway's northward flow.
Out of such places a double handful
of pine duff and ancient leaves
may leap every ten years or so
if you're lucky, its wings whistling,
or else you may see it at roadside
of an evening, solitary, bird for
the corner of the eye: woodcock:
never walking or running,
but perambulating
as though to some avian rhumba.

Or you'll listen, hair freezing on the instant,
as it climbs the mid-March twilight,
its courting music like
ice water dripping, but sweeter,
faster, and after the breakout
you may even find the shells in there,
heavily freckled, fragments
on a litter of sticks and leaves.

For themselves and their place keepers,
these tangles generate a binding
abundance, and for this morning's
oriole music that's embodied
in the bird's char and fire,
then echoed in a redstart male's
lesser black and orange in there,
the goldfinch flareups,
magnolia and Canada warblers
splashing firelight and shadow
on the leaf-turning shade
until you'd think the heat of all those
propositions would reduce
these thickets to their smoking roots.

LISTENING TO THE COURTSHIP DELIRIUM
OF THE GREAT HORNED OWLS

Nightly now, under the Snow Moon,
they are singing of Love as they understand it—
that big-ticket item that leaves us tongue-tied.
So their offspring will land with roof-thumps
over our heads, come next May, they sing it
as they were meant to, *basso profundo*
in moonwhite that magnifies leaf scutter,

for no reason at all recalling how,
in Dingle once, I stepped from a phone booth
into a swirl of long-stemmed bridesmaids
debouching from cars—O attar of petals,
dangerous pastels—and, shrunk to crocus height,
I was willing to be that tall forever.

So what if some critical strain of eighteen-wheeler
rips through these moments? That's what I asked the dark
last night when the owls woke me. So what if it happens
between that memory of bridesmaids and this one
of owls courting? Those old Greeks had it wrong:

to never have been at all, that would be worst,
to have missed these moments that arrived
unbidden merely because we were here,
never to have woven a lifetime of these
momentary joys into a life—

my dog Finnbarr, asleep on the deck one morning
while a nest-making titmouse plucked hairs from his back,
woke up and turned to the sun, unsurprised,
giving the bird more time to complete its mustache.

Or that moon out the kitchen window, a licorice wafer
fallen from the roll. Until, along its southeastern edge,
a thread of light began, never before in sixty years, maybe
never again, backlit with the silence of October dawn.

SOUL OF THE RIVER

Slipping around the bend
of an instant, a shy,
wingéd thing, a spindleshanks
for hanging a body on,
if the soul can be seen

when it takes on the color of river ice
or a wall of reeds, shapes itself
to a cedar, then to a place where bark
sloughed off a gray pine trunk,

and the river's never the same
river twice, but a mirror to the eagle's
passing rumor and the now-and-then
of geese jockeying down the air
to announce opening water,

then the soul is the river's constancy,
and you are the soul of the river,
great blue, always near,
even on this winter morning—a lobe
of southern air pushing in until it's April
or October for a few hours again—

ice on the river going, the last
snow under roadside
bittersweet and chokecherry
like edges of seafoam,
the marsh hawk up and hunting,

heron, and you've been hunting, too,
your wet footprints crossing the road,
three toes and a spur, like a line
of tree runes on the asphalt, until that wind
chopping up the bay arrives to erase them.

AN EXPLANATION

While you were
at the post office,
twenty-five-six-seven
quail flowed through
your garden, dividing
around the fish pool

while the dog, that
crypto-rationalist, lay
on the deck as though
nothing wonderful
were passing the lantana

and nodding through
the asparagus and right up
the path, innocent as
a nursery school class.

Even before I saw them
I knew by their plaintive
quirking who they were,
and came out afterwards
to see the path
dimpled with their passing,

which is why I'm
still here, whispering
at the threshold
of the woods.

A CONSTANT, A MYSTERY

First cries of the outriding crows were all business
    this morning, calling in their reserves, and across miles
the beach gleaners heard, and broke out of
    their stutter-steps along the tideline by Egg Island.

Inspectors of marshland came loping in, responding
    Indian file from every horizon, joined by
the roadkill crews whom I would evince against the piling

    of things upon things, were I given to prophecy.
They circled a merlin trapped in a pine top, more yet
    crying in, stirring their shadows into the maelstrom,
involving the trunks and leaves with themselves,

    and the shed's wall, maneuvers the early Horse Peoples
might have learned from that carousel of noise
    blackening around the hawk unclutching and clutching

its perch up there for a clear break through the mayhem,
    then the whole carousal pitched suddenly sideways downhill
after it. Here we have loons come south off the lakes
    a while, fallen silent as this November coast,

and all summer a great blue heron alighting, donating itself
    as a few more reeds to the marsh pond, but the crows are
a constant, one or two looping the loop in February

    to announce the first spring-seems-possible day,
while the flock ranges the branches, their voices applauding,
    heralding Canada geese overhead, and one eagle
riverine for a few hours in spring. The crows

    go on forever, pulling together out of divided labors
into the possibility of joy, or against the beak of
    necessity, though nothing I know can explain that one

I found dead on Corn Hill Road in winter, a single feather
blue as October decorating its chest, mystery
of the province of poetry.

SWALLOW

The only one
on this pond, all the rest
a flock composed of
her shadow and
her image on water

and, look, her other
shadow on sand
under water, away from
the black-leaf bottom
that's like so many
more swallows

she appears
to arrive at the far
leaf-shadowed end
before she's quite
left this end, revolving,
speeding the water,

her breeze notching
the chop to blue-black
wingtips, hurrying the pond
through its skinny
flume all morning.

A SYNESTHESIA

All for the female whose eye
is a glitter lost on us among husks
of bark and deadfall in those pines,
her dumpy suitor who has flown
his lovesickness up the continent
leaps into a spiral, corkscrews
atwitter up the air, a hundred feet,
two hundred up the March twilight,
more, his loopy overture widening.
Woodcock: crepuscular
bogsucker with eyes at the back
of his head, with a brain they claim
is in there upside down, enough
cause for a shorebird to take
to the woods. Shall only the properly
constituted make art, or did we just see
what we heard? Did those sounds
that began as though a fly fisherman
were stripping line from his reel
create the illusion that we saw it,
a dance at once absurd and holy
as he drops in a ragged chattering
zigzag back among those trees?

IN EGG TIME

All sixty-three of his years
we've been at this circling
of the planet together, this dog
and I lapping the high school track,
going gray about the face
at about the same rate. When I
begin multiplying the minutes
by average calories burned,
he lags and cuts across
the soccer field, telling me
to ease up. Redwings are trackside
in the reeds again. May. Three males
keep us in line from three
dogwoods, while the fourth takes
the sun on his back so we can't
find him, and stays up there
till we're out of nest range.
Not like the terns next month
on Egg Island, where we'll
come close to a furious barbering
all the way down the flats.
But I'd know that collar up ahead
anywhere: killdeer, first claimant
on this field when the grass
shakes winter off. Dragging
a corporal stripe away from some
pocket of earth that's warmed
to the rounding of things, this one's
trying to lead us off stride,
a wing-fake we won't
fall for, locked as we are
in our own distraction display.

GREAT HORNED OWLS

1

A log shifting in the grate,
or some onyx-eyed gnawer
dropping around for suet—
I snap to under goosedown,
my breath stilled
in the near frost of the room.

A few hours ago,
the last streaks of February
stacked in the cut between hills,
and our small marsh tilted and took in
the reedy blatting of geese,

and now, maybe down off
Cathedral Hill, an owl
begins her midnight blue vibrato,
like a sound before sounds,
a five-part respiration of the earth.

2

What consolation is it
that they mate for life,
the male bowing and scraping to her,
renewing his vows
in the bottom nights of each year?

His courtship gifts
are the whimper borne through the air,
the rabbit's imprint stopped
partway across snow,
and the bone spree slung as though
from a diviner's hand.

3

In March, motherly, she'll ride
the jumble of sticks and pelts
she bumped a hawk for,
warming her egg
though she's sodden as a stump.

Winds crossing April will flirt
in tail feathers harmless as a hen's,
until one afternoon she walks off,
pumping her five-foot span,
and begins doting on
the owlet that hisses her home
to pin it in crossed wings

and pass it the brains of
that flicker who strops his beak
on our tin chimney these dawns,

and the warbler whose song
will be amputated mid-run,
and the unlucky leaf-treader
whose squeal of outraged dignity
will flare like a stain
through sleep,

because, just now,
from across the marsh,
the male floated back that same
pentamorous call,
dactyl, trochee,
a tremolo stitching the small hours together.

WHIRL IS KING

Here and there
in the trees' understories,
that momentary thumbling's piping out
a helix of song

palpable as zebraic
black-and-white warblers
who tailgate each other,
running the bugs down, though

it's not one of them
or even a redstart
or parula that's
picked its way here

across consecutive dusks,
barely ahead of the air's
polar bulge. My eyes
dive through binoculars

till dimensions queue up,
then back off to focus
in time for a branch's
empty trembling. There

it is again. Be quick,
be quick, quicker than
the way one chickadee
appears to become two

who dive to admit
a third and suddenly
all change to a treeful of
olive-feathered fingerlings,

air-fish off in a single
upswing so I turn in a vortex
of my own, grabbing the rail
just before the misstep.

POEM OF THE TOWHEE

Peripheral leaf-shufflers,
they're a black stroke of
the Japanese brush
over a reddish, quietly
passionate streak.
This one has bunted the window
all spring, baffled by glass,
and now, over my head,
a gray, humped spider has set up
like a text creeper
before the poem the towhee
printed there in accents
grave and acute, in characters
beyond any translation.

ON THIS AFTERNOON OF MARCH 24

A piping plover fresh off this southern breeze
has walked into one of my footprints and assumed
a profile low enough to keep an eye on me.

I think of the minimal nests
they scratch out above the wrack line,
and how she threw the two ounces of herself

against cloudbanks, and navigated airstreams,
one of only a few thousand left, a trace element
of wide migrations no one will see again.

Unless she's one who will bring her kind
back from the edge, turning out clutch
after clutch of buff-colored eggs, spotted

dark brown and looking as natural
in this geology as inch-long stones the sea
has polished, one who will reverse

the work of market gunners and sportsmen
who went for the plovers after they
whipped the Eskimo curlews, then

posed napoleonic and custerly behind
mounds of least sandpipers.
Was I sent or dropped off here only to make

footprints for her, foxholes in the berm
between Egg Island and the bay,
where she goes a few feet, stops,

heads off on a tangent, pokes and feeds?
Is this what I'm for? Let it be
my *raison d'être* then, as good as any.

BACKTALK

Like a cross between a hinge
in need of oil and a girl
just learning to whistle,
all night you *shreep* out there,
little owl, maybe thirty feet
from the house. I float on
the surface of sleep, hearing you
wingclap around, a noisy hunter,
though somehow you manage
to turn off the voice of
a night wanderer in mid-chord.
When I let the dog out
at five A.M. you flap from
a tree six feet away; all day
you're somewhere in sight,
a new lump on the trunk of a pine,
or treed cat, stoic under
the black straggle of crows
you draw from miles around,
who know that later, when
your voice deepens into your chest,
you'll slip through their roost
snipping heads off. Meanwhile,
you've adopted our lamplit
domesticity, wanting to come in
where all week I've been trying
to write about choughs, rooks
and jackdaws who gather
in first light's rain around
Irish chimney pots and harangue
in peat-smoked gutturals
like their names—you drag me
home to the poetry under my nose.

LYING TO FALL WARBLERS

Little questions of eyestripe,
wing bar and tail covert,
seed herds of the boreal fields
and aspen parks,

you who know heights
above water so green
no grass conveys it,

if I could learn
your slow, wheezy,
and ascending songs,
master their downward slurs
on the penultimate note,

I would tell you
how one year I intend
to plant bull and wavyleaf thistle
for you alone,
where now my squash leaves flop
like elephant ears.

So what if, overnight,
mushrooms have boiled up
through plush,
anthracite and Mr. Potatohead
breaking down wood punk and leaf,

and a family of Indian pipes
wears peasant brown,
royalty turned out
of the summer palace?

When light slips south
along these natural threads
close to the ground,

let egrets nudge their young
from creek mouth to inlet
to warmer shallows.
What do they know?

Last night the Perseids
let stars go
in windfalls, and here you are,
ripe fruit filling the trees:
yellowthroat, blackpoll, bay breast,
flocks mixed as any
human motive,
names relearned for an hour.

Put by the urgency
we can't explain, and stay.
Teach *haute couture*
to the fish crow whose cry
is a New Year's horn
in his throat,
and manners to pinheaded jays.
Show chickadees
how to flare back at the sun.

Don't go skipping out
after that line of clouds
trotting east in light's
last tilt of rosé.

Night is a black wall,
and there are no Indies.
Stay here, under the steel edge
sweeping a way for rain.

OWL-STRUCK

Like some red-faced god
rummaging in a barrel,
wind was tossing sparrows
over dune rims.
A morning for firesides
and splitting emotional hairs,
but I went out under geese
Canadian as the front,
their necks tensed
to rudders, and met
a herring gull on the flats
who picked up my pace,
sighting over his shoulder
as if my being there
made things serious.
He was smoky blue
instead of oyster-shell,
maybe changed by air
snapping its whips and flags.
I stopped speculating
on a white D.P.W. fencepost
miles from any highway
when the snowy owl
swiveled its glare on me,
and remembered northern
routes, and spirits
with harvest-moon eyes
swimming in and out of
headlight snow. Owl-struck,
they call it. My blood tree
shook in wind trying
to flail the browns
from dunegrass, and the owl
flew, as if I could tell it
something it didn't want to hear.

A WINTER WREN

Vest-pocket troglodyte,
spelunker of hollow trees,
by your jitters we know you fear
the dangerous way

as we do, yet lead us
with your narrow face
like a hermit's
into the woodpile
where we cannot go.

You take us by your working
in among the splinters,
down one unlit corridor
then another, furtive
and mouselike,

as if that sustained warble
from your brain the size
of a teardrop makes up for
hollow bones and a frail beak,

equips you with the complexity
to show us the way
through this cord's solid oak
toward that jagged
measure of daylight.

A CAUTIONARY TALE

The way a scrub oak reaches
into itself to bring up
a little maroon-gone-to-copper
for its winter leaves,

one of these days, thinking
it's just as natural, you'll
reach in a pocket and come up
with a handful of sunflower seeds.

Like some gray rag-thaw
given up by old snow, wearing
slippers everywhere, taking
the newspaper only to stuff it
in cracks as, room by room,

the house comes down, you'll move
from one room to the next
just in time, with no facility
but the woods where bluejays
rip themselves from the sky
to eat your provender.

You'll see. Not Dr. Dolittle,
not even St. Francis will want
to look you in the eyes
for the oceanic sky that's
taken over in there, lined with
inklings of south-going flocks.

That one far deciduous tree
like a brain thinking in green
will do all your thinking then,
and you'll sit with hands folded
on silence, while the evenings

compose themselves in egret-egg
blue, shell greens of eider
and goldeneye, hues to prompt
the clutches in hidden nests,
if you keep on talking
to the birds the way you do.

TRANSMIGRATION

When your bones turn
loose and light as a deck chair
and you raise a rickety
blue pavilion over yourself,

beginning to see from above
how a breeze
ignites marsh grass every-which-way
to new greens,

at first fear will set you down
in the tip of an oak,
your new feet gripping.
Wait. Let instinct assure you
you look like only another
piece of sky between ragged trees.
So this is it.
Who would believe,
this late, this century . . .

You were running the low tide—
a man in midlife
trying to shake off a pelt
built of too many
trips to too many troughs,
rightly accusing yourself
of having sat out easy rains.

Printing the glacial till
back of Egg Island,
threading pincer movements
of tide, making gulls thrash
water to light, you were
changed in a battering
wink of their wing-storm.

Put everything away.
As if this tree could suddenly

haul in branches and leaves,
you can take in your new wings,
becoming all trunk,
a long-necked sapling
up to the sun.

Then one white stump-crouch
and spring, arms wagging
a quick blue semaphore,
going away until, flat out on air,
that looseness again,
the lattice of bones sliding
above sinews of creeks.

What are you, a soul?
It seems easy to push
earth off and be a diver
exempt from gravity, to flap out
above hay wastes and revolve till
the airport runway could be
a dropped paperclip,

or to glide, a shadow across
hogbacks, for the first time
seeing the art of tractors,
and ocean at practice whittling sandspits,
piling silt like reflected cumulus.

And those ponds back of town,
stations of glacial water
worked by an underworld of
shifting twilights,
permanently cold because
they were shed from the icecap's
orphaned bergs: Little Duck,

a mirage through pines,
where you found the wild wintergreen
and kept a leaf on your tongue,
wishing for deer all the way
to its white shore,

and Ryder, whose beach
you curled up on with one summer's girl
long ago, and woke to Billy Morna,
Old Man Newcomb, the whole road crew
staring over the bank
like kids around a barrel of strange fish—

though such memories are useless,
you find you can go there
and stand in the pale bole
of this new shape, indulging
your hunger for swimming food.

And when blue hollows
invite deeper blues, and marsh
takes on the aura of
undersea fields, last light
drops off the planet's
easy curve, though you rise
in juddering bones to keep it.

What's this? A voice up here?
Voices. Crackles of speech
as off a police radio,
some river of air alive with rage
tearing itself to froth.
Industrial sump, guggle of
money talk shot through
the redolence of a barbecue.

As you pass through the vowels
of love, scenting flowers
whose names, now, you will
never get straight, you know
you will come here often
for snatches of the inconsequential
that bind person to person
and day to day below,

where Main Street seems to be lifting
moonward, and headlights run
out a few capillary roads
among dunes grained
like the surface of old bones.
Veering, you scout for
a sour updraft of pond.

And in the end, come to yourself
above roofs struggling unequally
out of leaves. Hearing bells
crosscut by rifts of wind,
and an organ thin as a harmonica.

Lifted from that pattern
you can't feel for what you trail
above familiar cars up Main Street,
Commercial, School Street,
arriving over Memorial Lawn,

and nothing you could say
to that veiled woman
and downcast kids would explain
this simple rightness of things.

The wind shifts, and as if
in a time lapse, maples begin
flaunting their reds. Arranging
the town off one wing, and sea,
squalling up, off the other,

you hang out on air until
white, blue white, yellow,
the cloud-pelted moon
drags up new stars, magnitudes
winking out of the portside dark.

www.ingramcontent.com/pod-product-compliance
Lightning Source LLC
Chambersburg PA
CBHW031524270326
41930CB00006B/510